THE EARLY EXPERIMENTS

THANK YOU!

I'd like to extend my thanks to the following incredible people who supported Eclectic Projects via Patreon. Their support is a big reason this book exists.

Margaret Ball
Jodi
Nicole Strickland
Meg Vann
Sally Ball
Jennifer White
Maggie Slater
Tansy Rayner Roberts
Dave Versace
Mark Webb
Catherine Caine
Kathleen Jennings
Lois Spangler

Thank you all!

THE EARLY EXPERIMENTS
A SHORT FICTION LAB PRIMER

PETER M. BALL

Eclectic Projects (an imprint of Brain Jar Press)
PO Box 6687
Upper Mt Gravatt, QLD, 4122
Australia
Eclectic Projects: www.PeterMBall.com
Brain Jar Press: www.BrainJarPress.com

First published in Australia by Brian Jar Press 2018. This edition with new essay, Here Come The Boom, published 2023.

The Early Experiments 2nd Edition © 2023, 2018 Peter M. Ball. The stories in this collection were previous published in the following places, sometimes in slightly different forms and titles:

—"Upon Discovering The Ghost In the Five Star" copyright © 2016 by Peter M. Ball. First published in Daily Science Fiction, June 3rd, 2016

—"Counting Down" copyright © 2017 by Peter M. Ball. First published in Daily Science Fiction, March 3rd, 2017

—"The Place Beyond the Brambles" copyright © 2015 by Peter M. Ball. First published in Daily Science Fiction, November 5th, 2015.

—"The Things You Do When The War Breaks Out" copyright © 2016 by Peter M. Ball. First published in Daily Science Fiction, December 2nd, 2016

The moral right of Peter M. Ball to be identified as the author of this work has been asserted.

All rights reserved. No part of this book may be reproduced in any form or by any electronic or mechanical means, including information storage and retrieval systems, without written permission from the author, except for the use of brief quotations in a book review.

Cover design by Brain Jar Press
Cover Image: Bee Tattoo Art [intueri]/Shutterstock

ISBN: 978-1-922479-55-6 (Ebook) | 978-1-922479-56-3 (Paperback)

CONTENTS

Upon Discovering a Ghost in the Five Star	1
Counting Down	7
The Place Beyond The Brambles	13
The Things You Do When the War Breaks Out	19
Here Comes The Boom	25
On The Role of Inspiration In The Creative Process	
About the Author	37
Also By Peter M. Ball	39
Join the Eclectic Projects Patreon	41

UPON DISCOVERING A GHOST IN THE FIVE STAR

At first, I considered switching laundromats.

I mean, sure, the Five Star was just two blocks from my apartment, but there's something about a ghost girl by the dryers that takes the thrill out of throwing wet laundry in, paying your money, and settling into an ugly plastic chair to wait until the job's done.

Even worse, the Five Star used to get crowded in the afternoons. If you walked in and you were the fourth person there, you'd end up using the last dryer on the left, close to the spot she haunted.

Nobody wanted that. The closer you came to the ghost girl, the weirder it seemed to be there. She'd stare at you and offer the pink balloon tied to her wrist, and your skin attempted to peel its way free and get the hell away even if the rest of you insisted on staying put.

I stayed using the Five Star because she fascinated me as much as she frightened me.

Besides, the other laundromat was a good six blocks down the road.

The ghost had been Ella Sabine once. They beat her to death, in the back of the Five Star. Three punk girls with a grudge against

Ella's older sister. All charged for the crime, but they convicted only two. The third attacker avoided prison for another decade, eventually sentenced following a second lethal beat down in Tasmania. These kinds of things make the papers. You can track the details if you desire. Most people don't. We're too used to seeing ghosts. Too used to working round them, just another daily annoyance like taxes, traffic, and those asshole friends of a friend you're forced to encounter at said friend's parties.

The balloon piqued my interest at first. There are plenty of spirits in my patch of town, but few appear with accoutrements. I'd heard rumors about the ghost of an old highwayman, down on the corner of Sycamore, who still manifests his horse and sword, and a woman out by Starling Field who holds a ghostly lantern. Both were ancient hauntings, the legacy of an era when ghosts earned more respect and fear from the living.

These days we're lucky if a ghost manifests with pants to cover themselves, let alone a full ensemble and accompanying accessories. Ghosts, as with all things, are the victims of progress and the internet. We know too much about them, treat their hauntings like the tantrums of petulant toddlers thrown in a supermarket aisle. We take away the rewards that make ghostly existence bearable—attention and response.

There are more civilized ways of expressing displeasure than lingering—fueled by anger—for all eternity.

We tell ghosts this, over and over, until they look weak and blurry.

This one time, I visited the Five Star with my friend Maya and her girlfriend. I'd been telling them about the ghost girl and Maya wanted to see. Her girlfriend, Cassi Rollins, didn't appear to like Maya all that much. Cassi cracked jokes about Maya's eagerness to date other women, but they weren't really funny and never landed the way good in-jokes should. My impression, as we walked to the Five Star, suggested they'd been having problems.

It got worse, after we arrived there, 'cause Cassi goaded Maya into accepting Ella Sabine's balloon. She acknowledged it was stupid—we all knew it was stupid—but Maya did it anyway. She approached the ghost of Ella Sabine, wrapped her fingers around the length of pink ribbon. The ghost girl smiled, let go of the balloon, and Maya pitched backwards. Fell against the cracked tile in a shuddering, tooth-grinding seizure until we dragged her out the door and into the warm sunshine.

She recovered, but Maya lapsed into uncharacteristic silence afterwards. Pale and twitchy when I caught up with her on campus, avoiding contact with her students unless absolutely required by lecture times and scheduled office hours. Weeks later, after a faculty meeting in which Maya seemed disengaged, I cornered her to ask what occurred.

"I felt how Ella died," Maya said, really quiet.

"You know how it happened?"

"No," she said. "It's like her memories took up residence in my head. I felt what she felt, lying there in pain, waiting…"

Maya shuddered and looked away. I tried to get more out of her, but she no longer wanted to talk.

Her girlfriend left a few months later. Cassi claimed she couldn't take it anymore, the way Maya closed off. I think she saw an opportunity, decided it was time.

I did not mourn Cassi's departure, but Maya disappeared a few weeks after that. They emptied her office one afternoon and announced she'd taken leave, but that was a concession to the students who'd loved Maya's classes. Nobody really knew where Maya was and whether she planned to return.

My love life, honestly, seldom involves smarter choices than Maya. I'd been seeing this guy named Oliver when the ghost girl first appeared. He used to throw his dirty laundry in with mine, but he loathed the texture of clothing dried in Ella Sabine's proximity. "My underwear's haunted again," he said. "You did it near that ghost-chick, right?"

I told him no ghost-chicks were haunting his boxers, but Oliver refused to believe me. We broke up when he started complaining about the time I spent on research. "It's the ghost-chick or me," he said, one night, and I chose Ella Sabine.

A colleague at the university did his thesis about hauntings and the cultural methods we used to disenfranchise the ghosts and disempower them. He and I ate lunch together on Tuesday, escaping our students and campus politics, and he mentioned his thesis one afternoon while we dined at the off-campus sushi place.

"It's unfair to go out there and deny ghosts their anger," he said. "Historically, the designating proper and improper behavior has been a method of control for centuries. The privileged refuse to acknowledge legitimate grievances because of tone or impolite expression. They dub people too angry, too emotional, too Other, and suddenly the way they say it means more than what's said."

"I expect things are worse for ghosts," I said. "You know, compared to the living."

My colleague didn't agree with me.

"Disenfranchise any part of society, and they'll effectively disappear," he said. "Life and death doesn't mean shit, on matters of being silenced."

I quickly changed the topic and stole one of his gyoza, but I could sense his disapproval through the rest of the meal, even after I offered to pay.

If I were braver, I would have followed Maya's lead. Gone down to the Five Star, reached out my hand. Discover what sent my friend off the deep end, made her disappear and never return. Figure out, maybe, where she's fled, so I could bring her back before the university depleted its sympathy and her job was gone for good.

Instead, I hit the internet and searched for new details about Ella Sabine's death. News reports, abandoned MySpace accounts, anything that marked her passing. There's more stuff like that than you'd think, all the detritus we leave as we live our lives.

It never seemed to help.

I came closest to reaching for the balloon just after Oliver left me. I was drunk, and I stumbled into the Five Star with a pile of laundry, a hip flask of bourbon, and a sweater to ward off the cold. Forced myself to use the last dryer on the left, although it took half the booze before I summoned the guts to try. The ghost of Ella Sabine watched me approach, her head tilted to the side, dark hair falling across her pale, unsmiling face. Up close, I could make out the red smear of blood staining the side of her skull. They'd smashed her temple against the dryer door, repetitive trauma until the bone cracked. That much, at least, was in the news reports when I started digging.

I loaded wet laundry into the machine and she offered me her pink balloon.

I slipped on the tiles, scrambling backwards. A failed attempt to flee.

When Oliver left me, post-ultimatum, he couldn't figure out why I'd chosen Ella Sabine.

I tried to explain it, failed miserably. But then, I fail at many things.

These days, I use the laundromat six blocks down, and it isn't by choice, not really. They closed down the Five Star, in the end. People wouldn't use the dryers, not with Ella Sabine's ghost there. Not that they ever used that excuse—we know better than to admit we're afraid around a ghost—but that was the reason, no doubt about it. I tell myself I'm not relieved, that I would have been fine to keep going back there.

I go down to the Five Star once a year, on Maya's birthday. Use a crowbar to pry open the boards up front, light a candle in a cupcake to fight back the darkness. Ella Sabine's still there, down the back, near the ancient Maytag. I sit on a plastic chair and celebrate absent friends. I sing loud and off-key—that happens when I'm drunk.

Ella Sabine is always waiting for me, full and pale as ever.

Offering me her balloon, trying to communicate what she needs with her sad, dark eyes.

One day, I swear, I'll take it. One day I'll understand her pain, what keeps her whole and strong when other ghosts fade.

I got real good at lying to myself, as the years went by.

COUNTING DOWN

Phil says he can catch a bullet, and none of us believe him.

You have to know Phil: he says shit like this. The first night I met him, he swore he could backflip from a standing start. Bet me twenty bucks, and I put up the money. He got halfway over before gravity took over and he crashed into concrete.

We called an ambulance. They hauled Phil away. We returned to our party.

I ran into him a week later, and Phil showed me the stitches, a neat row above his eyebrow, straight like the seam of a shirt.

"That's an ugly one," I said.

Phil attempted to frown and flinched. "Yeah, but it could have been worse. My head is full of bats, you know? If they'd gotten out, that would have been awful."

I said, "Better to have them free, though, instead of leaving them in there?"

Phil blinked. Then he grinned. "I like you," he said.

He gave me a twenty, fair is fair, because I'd won our bet.

And so I became Phil's friend, and learned you can't get rid of him.

. . .

The bullet thing is new. And this time, Phil's adamant, swearing black-and-blue he can snatch a shot from the air. It's not a good idea to believe him. Phil's been drinking. Hell, we're all pretty buzzed right now. When Angie holds a party, all of us fucking drink. And plenty of people will take him up on the offer to shoot him, if Phil's got a gun.

No, not *if*. I know he'll have one. Phil commits. He throws himself into things. "For real," he says, "I can totally do it. Somebody grab my Luger."

When nobody goes, he calls us all a pack of assholes, gets the damn gun himself.

Daphne says she'd be down with shooting Phil. She says it quiet, in my ear, low enough that I'm the only person who hears. I'm glad of that, I really am, the fact she's only willing to share that thought with me. There're many folks here who are tired of Phil's shit. All sorts of people who figure, what the hell, let the goddamn asshole get shot, you know?

People who'd take what Daphne said and use it to egg her on, put the Luger in her hand and make her take fifteen paces before pulling the trigger.

It was Phil who introduced Daphne and I. Three years back, at another party. We owe him for that. Together, it's been three years of happiness. Or, you know, as close to happy as relationships get. Phil claims it wasn't his idea. The bats told him to do it. I don't care. We owe Phil, or we owe the damn bats. They're both walking around in the same goddamn skin.

I don't want to shoot him, and I don't want Daphne to do it either. If it's Phil we owe, I want him alive. You don't repay friends with gunshots.

If its bats we owe, I want them kept inside his skull. After what I'd seen, I sure as hell don't want the bats out here.

· · ·

You may have surmised this already, but I'd like to make it clear: Being Phil's friend isn't easy.

I know. I've been Phil's friend for six years now, and there's always shit like this going down. He used to do this trick with knives. First, he wanted to throw them at you. Told you he could do it clean, had real steady hands. No-one was stupid enough to say yes, until our friend Mandy said sure, stood against the wall and posed.

"Come on," she said. "Get it over with. Money where your mouth is, yeah?."

And Phil, he went to work. Put three knives into the plaster, all tight and snug against Mandy's arms. We started to believe his shit, a little. I mean, he was drunk, but he was pulling it off.

Then he put the forth blade into the meat of Mandy's leg, staggered over to the window and threw up in the garden.

Mandy fell, screaming blue murder. She wasn't alone in that. Once again, we called the ambulance, but her departure put a dampener on the rest of the party.

We were all aware of Phil's presence, the threat that he might want to try his trick again if he sobered up.

Phil tells women he grew up in a circus. Says he learned this shit from his mother, a knife-thrower, and the acrobat she'd been dating through his pre-teen years. Phil lacked the passion to follow in either of their footsteps as a pro, but he developed a knack for both their arts. Picked up work as a clown for a summer job. Learned to make a crowd laugh, or at least pretend to laugh.

And I'll say this: Phil can pratfall like a motherfucker. He does it for fun, while shopping. One minute he's walking the cereal aisle, the next he's on the ground. People rush over, worry about his health.

Store managers run over, worried he'd try to sue them.

Then Phil gets up, laughing. Swearing everything is fine. "Just clumsy," he tells them. "No-one's fault but mine."

He does it because he likes the attention. The commotion and the fear, the way folks bustle around him.

. . .

Phil says it hurts sometimes, having a head full of bats. He claims he does shit 'cause he needs a distraction, a few seconds of external stimuli louder than what occurred inside his skull.

He says it's the only escape he's got, outside of a bottle of scotch.

Daphne used to say we fell in love at first shirt. Because she wore a Lou Reed *Transformer* shirt, the first night we met, and I wore a *Meat is Murder* shirt I'd stolen from my older brother. We bonded over eighties pop, after Phil introduced us. We talked, we flirted, we friended each other. It still took me three weeks to ask Daphne out, and even then Phil goaded me into it. He listened to me talk and, one day, he snapped and delivered an ultimatum.

"Throw this knife at me, motherfucker," he said. "If I catch it, you sack up and you ask her. Otherwise, you stop telling me about her, dig?"

Phil and I were sharing a flat that year. He badgered me until I gave in and threw the blade. He caught it, won the bet, and I called Daphne the next day.

Fair is fair, after all.

And that's how we ended up here.

When Phil likes a girl, he falls back on what he knows. Mostly, that's drinking, and a bunch of carnival shit. This one time, to impress a girl, he hammered a six-inch nail up his nostril. Pulled it off okay, but there were nose bleeds for two weeks after.

This one time, to impress a girl, he threatened to pull a live bat out of his ear. Gave her the whole damn spiel. "I can hear them all the time," he said. "Squeaking and flapping around in my skull."

Of the tactics, the nail worked out better for him.

And, even then, it didn't work out better by much.

. . .

This one night, a week back, I stayed at Phil's place. He was drunk; I was drunk. It seemed like a good idea. I crashed out on his couch, woke around three and stumbled to the bathroom, wondering if I would puke. Phil's voice seeped through his bedroom door.

There weren't any words in what he was saying, but there was a rhythm, like poetry, undulating and strange. It gave me an ugly feeling. I knocked on Phil's door. Checked on him, when he didn't wake.

It's February and hot as hell in Brisbane. I learned Phil slept naked, when I sat down by his bed.

The muttering stopped. Phil's eyes stayed closed, and he lay there, very still, a sheet tangled around his legs, covering his junk. When he spoke, his voice sounded very, very far away.

Phil said, "Mattie?"

Then: "Mattie, you can't be in here."

"Dude," I said. "I just wanted—"

Phil opened his eyes and looked at me. They weren't the eyes I recognized. They were dark and endless, black like polished marble. I could see things, in behind them. Bats, maybe, just flitting about.

Or, you know, not bats at all.

Nothing like bats, not really.

"You shouldn't be here," he said, real quiet, and he didn't sound like Phil anymore. I got the hell out of there, caught a cab home. Told Daphne nothing about it.

Now Phil's walking around the party, looking for volunteers. He goes past me and Daphne twice, looks me in the eyes both times. Decides and comes back to me, pushes the Luger against my chest. "Mattie," he says, "You're designated shooter."

Daphne squeaks, beside me, like she's realized that he's serious.

"Phil, man, come on," I say. "We believe you. You don't have to do this."

He leans over, and he hugs me. "It's going to be okay," he whispers. "I swear, it'll be okay."

"Phil," I say, "I really don't know."

"Come on." He glances in Daphne's direction. "You owe me. You know you owe me."

"Ladies and gentlemen," Phil says, every inch the showman. "Please, for your own safety, don't try this at home. And please, for the sake of your defense attorney, only help out when you're drunk."

People laugh. They're used to laughing at Phil. He's a funny guy. He turns towards me, spreads his arms wide. Takes a step back, all smiles.

Another step. Another. Fifteen paces in total.

"I'm counting back from ten," he says. "When I'm done, you shoot."

I shake my head, say nothing.

"Aim here," Phil says. Puts a finger against his temple. "Don't worry. I'll catch the bullet. Not going to hurt me at all."

He lowers his hand and takes a deep breath. Steadies himself with a nod.

"Ready?"

I'm not. I'm totally not.

"Ten." He smiles. His eyes turn black. I can see them moving inside his skull.

"Nine," he says. "Eight… seven… six…"

And me? I lift the gun.

THE PLACE BEYOND THE BRAMBLES

When last I saw you, my sweet, my love, you'd shrunk to the size of Grandma's thimble, plucked from the porch by the bees of the forest. We heard your cries, your wild shrieks of delight, as they carried you to the place beyond the southern brambles. Listened, after, to the silence that followed, to the empty fields and the dark shadows beneath the trees where no bee remained to hum its evening song.

You've been gone a five-month, and Grandma does not know your name anymore, nor does Jordy or Cousin Ferdinand or our dear, sweet Claudette. Whatever magic was used to shrink you, to make your final exit possible, stole all memories of you from those you once deemed as close as family.

But I still recall everything about you, my love, just as I remember your delighted squeal upon being taken aloft, just as I can summon the tiny hymn of joy on your lips as you fled to the place where I cannot follow. I know the contours of your face, burned into my mind on the first day we met, when you emerged from the forest in your dress of black and gold, and we conversed for hours and days on end, talked until you kissed me and declared that we would be lovers.

You tasted of honey that day, my love: so sweet; so sultry; so wild.

. . .

For those who prefer the technical term, you were taken by *Aspis mellifera*, the common honey bee. The Latin fascinated you, the first time you encountered it. You had me trace its genus in my books, explain the origins of the word. *Aspis:* bee. *Melli:* honey. *Ferre:* to bear. A designation proposed by Carolus Linnaeus in the eighteenth century, who later realized his mistake and tried to correct it.

In that respect, my sweet, my love, he is a smarter man than I.

People ignored his calls to use *mellifica*—maker of honey—in place of his first attempt. They did not care that it was inaccurate after growing used to the first nomenclature. Others did not fret about incorrect designations, nor comprehend the need to correct such an insignificant error.

Sometimes, in your heart, you understand things to be true, even if they are also wrong.

When we married, my sweet, my love, you carved a slice of our wedding cake and took it to the brambles. You left it there, that the bees would learn of your happiness, and spread news of it through the world.

We held our reception in the barn, danced across the dusty wooden floor and ate of the feast Cousin Ferdinand prepared, served on those great trestle tables laden with cakes and roast meats and pies. We did not own those tables, my love. Ferdinand acquired them from generous neighbors, much as he brought in the food and drink by calling upon those who owed him favors.

People thought highly of my family once, leastwise around these parts.

We had oft discussed what it must be like in the place beyond the brambles. I suspected you of being a bee-wife, right from the beginning, even though you promised otherwise. We each told Claudette different tales about the kingdom of the hives. In mine, the bees inhabited a golden land, serving the Queen with a slavish devotion. Beyond the brambles there were rivers of honey and flower-covered hills, vast swathes of clover where the bees could rejoice and play.

In your stories, the land beyond the bramble was merely another bee-hive. Bigger. Grander. More impressive. You saw no need to personify, held no truck with suggesting magic as an idyllic force in their lives.

"Why should the bees conform to your human desires?" you asked me. "Must you make strange things so familiar before you can appreciate their beauty?"

I call Claudette our daughter, but I know this child is not truly mine. No get of a bee-wife's womb will ever belong to their father.

Claudette shares your hair, your smile, your face. She shares your penchant for walking the fields, letting the bees gather around her. She shares your knack for speaking to the swarms, coaxing them into a conversation.

Occasionally the bees sting her, but Claudette doesn't cry out.

The bees are hers, as they'd once been yours, and I fear they will take her as well.

I am not a foolish man, my love. I knew, when we married, that it would be forever.

The men of our village accept brides from the forest. Nettle brides and fox brides and daughters of the elm and the willow and the river. They are often beautiful, always enchanting, and none have ever stayed for long. They come, they marry, they bear us children, and then the trees reclaim them.

We do not speak of it, not in the open, but it's common knowledge such things happen. When you disappeared, oh my love, people came to our door to pay their respect. The delivered foods—frozen blocks of casserole to defrost and microwave—and said nothing about your origins.

"Be pleased you've got your daughter," they told me. "Claudette, she is a bonnie girl."

I ask about you, to prompt some lingering recollections, but their memories are fading, or faded and gone.

This, too, I expected, given who you were.

I make lists of the things I no longer recall: your name; our first words on the day we met; the exact and specific color of your eyes on the evening of the summer storms.

That thing you told me, that morning. The one before you went away.

I make lists of the things I remember still: we can measure the average life of a worker bee in months. Weeks sometimes, in colder climbs, where winters are long and cruel. The average lifespan of the Queen gets measured in years, often four, but sporadically longer.

I never learned your age, my love. We did not celebrate birthdays in our house.

I do not know if you're alive or dead, although I keep hoping for one or the other.

I spend the evenings on our back deck, my love, watching the brambles and the forest and the stars. I drink beer and write these letters, never quite sure where to send them, and I pretend that somewhere out there you can yet hear me and remember us as we were.

Some nights, when the sky is clear, Jordy comes out to join me. He is older—his brown skin worn to leather—and haunted by the same look that I recognize in the mirror now. He sits with me a while, and brings me a fresh beer, and the earthy scent of the field is replaced by the lilac of Jordy's hair tonic and the mint of the gum he chews.

Jordy married a fox-wife, I think. I do not recall her exactly.

"The hardest part," he tells me, "is getting used to memories that no-one else has. Treasuring them, 'cause they need to be treasured, without assuming that you've gone mad.

You loved her most, so you remember. That's the husband's burden."

And I would ask about his wife, if it would not pain him, for I've asked about her many times and I cannot keep her name straight in my head. There is something about her, as there is something about you, my love, that makes it difficult for those who weren't lovers to recall her.

Once, while very, very drunk, Jordy offered some darker advice.

"The hardest part isn't that everyone else has forgotten her," he said. "It's the dread, one day, that you'll find another man who remembers every detail."

I never asked him about this statement. I've never had the stomach. I cannot remember the woman he speaks of, so any comfort I offer is platitudes and conjecture.

But the fear of it sticks, like a knife to my gut. I can endure much, knowing I must endure it, but the thought you might have loved another wounds me beyond all measure.

I picture you there now, my sweet, my love, in the place beyond the brambles. Often I picture it, in my mind's eye, a reminder of you and where you've gone. A reminder that, yes, you are most likely happy, certainly happier than I could make you in this worn down house, on the border between the fields and the forest and the thorns.

I imagine you on a throne, my love, because I would not care to see you otherwise. This way, at least, I can pretend your departure is as much about duty as anything else. I console myself with a greater good, even if it is one I cannot understand.

I imagine you on your throne in a dress of gold and black and green, ruling your apiary subjects with kind words and a smile that soothes the soul like honey in hot tea. I picture your court with its busy rulers and its stiff, unyielding guards.

In my mind's eye, my love, my beloved, my only, I can see the rolling fields filled with clover. I can see the vast and endless hills covered in wildflowers.

. . .

This is the story I tell our daughter when she asks after her mother. You would not like it, my sweet, my love, but it comforts her more than science and truth. It comforts her more than tales of hives.

At least, it does for now.

THE THINGS YOU DO WHEN THE WAR BREAKS OUT

Your stomach does this funny lift, when they first activate the anti-grav. Nothing crazy, like you'd get if you were on a roller-coaster, but my dad, he was never a roller-coaster guy. Dad fixated on the idea the train's destined to crash, clutched the arm-rests with both hands and focused on his breathing to ease his nerves. Shallow breaths, in-out, in-out. Over and over for the whole thirty clicks it took to rise into low orbit.

"Dad, it's fine. We're protected," I said. "Nothing's going to happen to the train, okay?"

My father wasn't having a bar of it. "Your mum claimed that, prior to her first trip up. Perfectly safe, she said, and ever since she came back… well, you can't say it didn't affect her, eh?"

"Dad—"

He was breathing again. Ignoring me. My mother, she ventured to space early when the trains were still a new thing. She left my old man not long after she returned to earth, ran off with a bloke who worked at her office. Dad found see a connection between the two events. The rest of us couldn't. Mum claimed she could not hack it with dad, after things got rotten, and there wasn't any reason to doubt her.

Some days, I can't really hack it either. I feel ashamed, admitting that, but it remains the truth.

Still, Dad became calmer once we passed the Karman line and entered the thermosphere. You can see the dinosaurs from there, all the space-faring pterodactyls that flit toward the train like moths drawn to a light.

Dad said, "It's amazing, isn't it? Seeing them out there?"

And it was, I suppose, from his point of view. They were still extinct when he was a kid. Dad remembers the first encounter, after we ventured into space for real. They were hanging out on the dark side of the moon, waiting for us to come catch up and join them.

He always loved dinosaurs, my dad. Wanted to call me Rex, when I was born, except mum refused. She named me Henry and figured I'd turn out okay, with a sensible name like that.

Things went wrong. Of course they did. You finally take your dad into space, despite his protestations. You catch the train up—safest way to travel, everyone always says so—and you get him a good look at the creatures he loves and maybe, you think, he'll soften a bit. With luck, he'll finally stop holding onto this thing with mum and live his life a little.

So, yeah, of course, that's the day that the dinosaurs go mental, start swooping your carriage, snapping their beaks against the windows. Big noise, that. Loud as a gunshot. One crack, then another, and it brings back memories of a chick breaking free of an egg, 'cept this time they're getting in, not fighting their way out.

Thing is, it's not my dad who freaked out about it. "This is brilliant," he said. "They're like bloody magpies."

They weren't. They were big, leather-winged, and dangerous. They could survive in space, and we could not. I lapsed into the breathing thing this time, while my dad got his phone out and took a photograph.

"Dad," I said, "this is serious. They're trying to get in. They don't ordinarily—"

He shushed me, just like he did when I was a kid, speaking out of turn on a trip to a museum or library. The lights in the carriage turned red, and a polite voice informed us we should put on our seatbelts. A pterodactyl beak snapped against the glass right next to my head.

"Seatbelts," Dad said, and pointed at mine, as if I'd somehow missed the announcement. Then he twisted back to the window, cell phone in hand, and took another photo.

The polite voice returned, asking us not to worry. They planned to turn up the anti-grav, try to make a run for it.

There were dents in the side of our carriage when we disembarked at VS Station. There were soldiers in blue caps, guns slung against their hips, keeping a wary eye on the sky. One of them caught me and dad studying at the pitted marks, informed us we'd gotten lucky. "The two-fifteen out of Belfast," he said, "she's a good three hours overdue. 'Dactyls knocked her off-course, sent her drifting into irregular orbit."

We thanked him and hurried off the tarmac. Met up with my sister, who'd come out to greet us, after hearing about the attack on the news.

"Be an interesting visit," she said. "They're paying all sorts of attention about what's happening on the dark side. Nobody's mentioned evacuation yet, but it's on everyone's mind."

I sat in the back seat. My dad, up front, cycled through his photographs. He regaled my sister with enthusiastic details of the attack. "When we get home, I'll show you the pictures," he said. "Your brother was worried, silly duffer. Missed the chance to get all sorts of good shots of 'em up close."

"You were scared too, when we took off," I said.

"I," Dad said, "was apprehensive. Not the same thing at all."

They sent tanks into the dark side of the moon the following evening. My dad did not approve, but then he was an apologist. "Bloody ecological tragedy," he said. "Shouldn't be messing with their habitat like that, eh?"

My sister didn't agree.

"You're not from here," she said. "You don't really know what they're like. They're dangerous."

"Ecological tragedy," my dad repeated. He would not budge on that point. Trudged outside and taught her kids how to play Tyrannosaur. The game hadn't changed since I was a kid. He'd snarl and growl and chase them around, then fall over and go extinct when my niece pretended to be a comet.

My sister called him a stubborn old bugger. She made a fresh pot of coffee.

"How is he?" she said.

"He's good."

"No." She relinquished the coffee pot, placed both hands on the counter. "I mean, how is he, really?"

"Well, you know."

She nodded as if she truly did, and her assumption irritated me. She'd not seen my father in the flesh for the better part of a year, too distracted by her own her life to understand how poorly things progressed.

One of the soldiers came to my sister's door; a tall woman in a blue cap, blonde hair pulled into a tight, controlled bun. The soldier carried a gun slung over her left shoulder, her preferred weapons a stern, commanding tone and a sour expression. She informed us the war was not going well. Then made it clear we'd need to be ready to evacuate, if the dinosaurs advanced.

My father disappeared that evening, sneaking out after we'd gone to bed. My niece found a note on his pillow the next morning: *Heading to the dark side. Not coming back. I'm sorry.*

The soldier returned and took our report. She stressed, very clearly, no one should go after him.

We followed Dad. Of course we did. He might be going bonkers, but he was still our father. My sister called in some favors, got us let out past the city limits in this beat-up old rover. Stayed on the ground, skulked through valleys every chance we could.

Avoided open spaces, kept a wary eye out for pterodactyl's above.

"This is your fault," my sister said. "He would have been bloody content on Earth. I would have brought the kids to see him."

"You wanted him to visit," I said.

My sister's lips were a pale, tight line.

"We should have known this would happen," she said. "Dinosaurs were always going to be trouble."

"It's been fifty years," I said. "Nobody predicted this."

We fell silent, the two of us. Evacuation was due to start within six hours. If we weren't back, we stayed behind. Her wife would get the kids away, keep them safe on the trains.

Then dinosaurs found our rover, seven clicks out.

Your stomach does this funny lift, when your buggy gets attacked while you're traversing the surface of the moon. Sharp beaks rap against the thick layers of glass and you hear your sister screaming. No calm voice to explain the situation, just panic and terror and the heavy crash of your own heartbeat. Deep breaths won't relax you. If the cabin cracks, deep breaths are not really advised.

Things are going very wrong.

You think about your dad, alone on the dark side of the moon. You recall those trips to museums to study bones. You think about playing Tyrannosaur and how you squealed, as a boy, when he chased you.

You think about your mum, and how long it's been since you saw her.

You think about the crack on the windshield, getting longer. The hiss of oxygen escaping. The engine whining as you try to run, your sister screaming something about sealing the system.

You think about all the ways you could have helped your father, and didn't. The trip to the moon was supposed to improve things.

It hasn't.

And you think, *it will work out. There's got to be another chance.*

And you think, *this is amazing, look at them all out there.*

And you think, *that crack is getting bigger.*

And then you do the breathing thing. In-out. In-out.

Make use of the air remaining, in the time you've got before it runs out.

HERE COMES THE BOOM
ON THE ROLE OF INSPIRATION IN THE CREATIVE PROCESS

"WHERE DO YOUR IDEAS COME FROM?"

Ask where ideas come from, and some author will make fun of you.

It feels inevitable because writers are supposed to loathe this query, and I'm often dismayed at the folks who lean into the myth. Authors who reach for the barrage of ready-made quips and responses designed to chastise those who dare ask the question, ranging from referencing an ideas-of-the-month club or little shops in Schenectady, through to the gentle rebuke this is the one question you must never ask a writer. I've seen authors at the top of their game do this—thirty years into their career and deceptively knowledgeable about the craft—and new authors pick up the ball and follow their example.

Even so, people keep asking, and writers continue to hedge with their answers. When that happens—and, if you're at a writing event where someone asks, it surely will—please remember this: most professional writers shrug the question off because the answers are rarely magic or insightful. Ideas are just ideas, plentiful as sand on the beach and about as ordinary.

I can tell you the initial spark for every story in *The Early Experiments*, but I suspect it will disappoint most folks.

Upon Discovering A Ghost In The Five-Star emerged from a

Friday Flash Fiction challenge Chuck Wendig posted on his site, which features a random image of a spooky girl with a red balloon. I picked the setting because I'd been meaning to write a series of speculative fiction laundromat stories since 2009[1], and I wanted to get at least one out of my system.

Counting Down had its origins in a social media meme—one of those recurring exercises in firing up the music player, hitting shuffle, and responding to the first song. Mine was The Birthday Party's punk classic, *Release the Bats*, and I flashed back to the time a group of friends and I got stuck in Brisbane overnight (It's very hard to leave a Goth club when *Release the Bats* comes on, even if it means you're going to miss the last train home for the night). What should have been a Facebook post became a story seed instead.

I wrote *The Place Beyond The Brambles* in response to an open call from the Brisbane-based Tiny Owl Workshop, who asked for tales inspired by twelve images sketched by artist Terry Whidborne. My submission didn't make it into the final project, but it was picked up by *Daily Science Fiction* a year later.

Finally, *The Things You Do When The War Breaks Out* responded to a post-it sketch from my friend Kathleen Jennings, which was itself something of an in-joke revolving around dinosaurs and Terrence Haile's *Space Train*. For years, Kathleen had been doing illustrations based on friend's stories, so I figured I'd return the favour. Problem is, I have no talent for art, so I wrote a story to go with her drawing instead.

I think we can agree there's no magic there, but here's the thing about inspiration: *it's the least interesting aspect of a story*. The raw idea is a lit match capable of igniting the bundled dynamite we call a great story, but it needs someone who can pack the explosives, spool out the long fuse, and deliver a controlled (or semi-controlled) kaboom.

Without that, you're just an asshole with a lit match and nothing to set on fire.

LIGHTING THE FUSE

My favourite model for how writer's develop comes from the science fiction writer Samuel Delany, who breaks a talent for story into two parts: first, the aspiring writer absorbs a series of complex models around constructing sentences, developing characters, achieving believable plots, developing a satisfying narrative, and seeking rewarding publication, which the author internalises to the point they're almost subconscious.[2] Second, the aspiring writer learns to submit to these models, enduring their strictures and limitations as they shape one's narrative impulses. As Delany puts it:

> *The sad truth is there's very little that's creative in creativity. The vast majority is submission—submission to the laws of grammar, to the possibilities of rhetoric, to the grammar of narrative, to narrative's various and possible structurings.*
>
> *ABOUT WRITING, P. 121*

This model's discussed in Delany's seminal book on the craft, *About Writing: Seven Essays, Four Letters, & Five Interviews*, which is perhaps the most dense and nuanced interrogation of authorship that I've come across in twenty years of writing and academia. It's also the exact wrong thing to tell a crowd of aspiring writers, who are often deeply invested in creative pursuits as confirmation of desired identity. All too often they're courting a self-image marked by creative freedom, hedonism, and rejection of normalcy, rather than a career spent embracing constraints and submission.

I don't blame them for that misconception because there's a mythology around writing and other art stretching back to the ancient Greeks. A notion that all art emerges from a source beyond the creator, bestowed by the muses and transformed into art by a process of rhapsodic and unconscious creation. In this model, inspiration is the primal wellspring from which great works flow, and we denigrate artists as flawed and unreliable vessels hand-picked to translate the divine.

We may not believe in the twelve Greek muses anymore, but their legacy remains. A quick survey of popular culture will reveal an endless succession of characters whose success is the product of innate genius or manic creative energy instead of a work ethic and diligent acquisition of skill. From the offbeat insights of *Castle*'s Rick Castle, better at solving murder than the NYPD detectives trained for the job[3], to the whole-of-life transformation of George McFly in *Back To the Future*, to the paralysed-by-writers-block Hank Moody in *Californication*, film and TV is full of authors with fates sealed (or doomed) by the quality of their ideas rather than their capacity for diligent progress and iterative development.[4]

Alas, the real world is no better. Culturally we lionise the "creative genius" and the inevitability of their success. Artist are free to work hard, so long as the work punishes them, eroding physical or mental health or pushing them to addiction. Those whose work is too prodigious or created with commercial intent are assumed to be lacking in inspiration and worth.

In this model Hemingway becomes a heavyweight of the literary canon, while James Patterson is a writer of pulp trash, despite Patterson's penchant for a sparse narrative style which uses a voice as prominent and distinct as Hemmingway's terse prose. The same dynamic sees the prolific Joyce Carol Oates acknowledged as a literary dynamo, while genre authors such as Nora Roberts off as scribblers of popular pulp, simply because Roberts writes popular fiction.

Dig down and the creative works of Oates and Hemingway use the same structures and tools as Patterson and Roberts. They may deploy them to different ends, for distinctly separate audiences, but the conventions of story are not so unique that you can't recognise them in play in every book. It's not the quality of their *inspiration* that differentiates these authors, but the way both writer and publisher position their work, and the interests of the readers they court.

In speculative fiction, the fallacy of inspiration is exposed with every themed anthology—I can give a dozen writers the same story prompt and end up with a dozen very different stories. What differentiates them isn't the inspiration that triggers the story, but the works each author immerses themselves in while building their models, the techniques and market awareness they bring to the table, and their particular mix of goals and ambitions that drive them to write.[5]

It would benefit everyone if writers admitted this freely, but that's not the world we live in. I've brought Delany's concept of submission up in countless classrooms full of aspiring and semi-pro authors, and some of them get seriously cranky at the notion that writing isn't a magical playground where muses fire concepts into your brainpan and allow you to make millions off the back of inspiration alone. Others are quieter in their distemper, grappling with the legacy of cultural programming that says you're either a literary genius or a peddler of cheap hack work, and fighting the realisation that having to put in effort positions them in the wrong camp.[6] When faced with a crowd pre-programmed to dislike the honest or nuanced answer, deflection is a natural impulse.

There's also a perplexing irony at play: to speak too freely of craft and effort, rather than vision or genius, is to invite denigration of the creative product. A writer can alienate readers with a nuanced answer about craft, and few authors are in a position where they want *less* people to read their work.

THE BURNING FUSE

The works in this primer emerged from specific prompts, but they turned into stories through an iterative process that developed the ideas, captured the voice, and ultimately shaped and re-shaped the narrative. Describing how this takes place is harder to describe than the original inspiration, and more idiosyncratic than many writers would prefer. For all the debates about plotting or pantsing—essentially the choice between writing off the cuff or laying out details before the draft beings—working writers cobble together an arsenal of tricks and techniques that play to their individual strengths and interests.

My process runs something like this: I spend the early stages of the writing process searching for the *frisson* that ultimately powers my interest.[7] A small detail, ambition, or pleasure that shows me *why* I'm pursuing the story, then sustains my attention when I find myself mired in drafts that refuse to click into place.

This aesthetic shiver rarely emerges from plot or character, nor does it need to be there when I first put words on the page. It's often easier to take a simple concept—I'll write a story about dogs—and *search* for the frisson as I go, running through aesthetic questions about the voice, structure, and style. Often, it's born from absurdity or contrast that defies conventions or norms in my chosen genres.

Nor is the frisson consistent throughout the creative process. Stories take time to develop, and the half-life of excitement varies. Once gone, the first source of frisson naturally hands off to another, and so on. I sustained the early drafting of *Upon Discovering A Ghost In The Five-Star* through the pleasure of merging a fantastic setting with the mundane setting of a coin-operated laundromat, which soon handed off to the pleasures of figuring out the rhythms and quirks narrator's voice.

The frisson powering *Counting Down* wasn't in the original seed at all—while drafting, I stumbled over an article about an illusionist doing a bullet-catching trick, which reminded me of an old acquaintance from my goth club days. He was a gamer whose stoned obsession with late night *Streetfighter* and *Tekken* tournaments bled into the real world, mutating into boasts about about doing backflip kicks or blocking swords with his bare hands. My short stint writing for theatre gave me some other details to play with, including a party where a street performer took great pleasure in doing very realistic pratfalls while drunk and generating panic among bystanders.

That combination gave me a voice, and the voice gave me an opening line: *Phil says he can catch a bullet, and none of us believe him*. Once established, the first line narrowed down the forking paths of narrative possibility, and experience filled in details— Phil's claim means someone needed to pull the trigger, and prove him right or wrong. Which begat a fresh round of questions: why would a reader care about the result, given Phil is just a noun rather than a living person? Who can pull the trigger, and why does it matter to them? Why does Phil want to try this in the first place? Each answer gave me new details, like carving away a block of marble to expose the statue within.

The frisson driving *The Place Beyond The Brambles* was the attempt at a fairy tale-esque narrator, but the story became interesting once I started describing the kingdom of bees and realised that making it less magical and more scientific gave me the contrast I was craving.

And the frisson that first pushed *The Things You Do When The War Breaks Out* lay in the absurdity of combining dinosaurs and levitating trains, but it fizzled in several drafts. It wasn't until that silliness handed off to the pleasures of writing about dads[8], playing against a much-loathed book, and figuring out the family dynamic that I discovered traction on the story.

These may suggest a muse in action to some, but my process has more common with Delany's notion of submission than it seems at first blush. My search for a frisson capable of powering a story is often driven by one of the largest and most complex models a writer engages with—the contemporary marketplace for fiction at the time they're writing—and my educated guesses about what will interest an editor.

I write the way I do, searching for the kinds of frisson that I enjoy, because it seemed like the easiest route to producing stories that will sell to editors I respect and find readers who'll appreciate them.

THERE WAS SUPPOSED TO BE AN EARTH SHATTERING KABOOM

Of course, ideas and frisson are only a minor aspect of selling a story. Execution matters, and that's where the skill and hard work come into play. For example, a few years ago I had an idea I figured for a winner: I would write a series of stories using techniques, practices, or resources that weren't part of my usual approach, then draft an author's note about the lessons I pulled from the process.

Over time, the collected writings would interrogate the creative process with more nuance than I could deliver in a classroom or book on writing. Rather than talking in general terms, the series would break down the toolkit that turned a concept like "ghost with balloon + set in a laundromat" into a story worthy of being reprinted and translated into other languages. More importantly, I could make overt connections between the inspiration that seeded the story and the techniques needed to generate a finished work.

Essentially, the series would be aimed at aspiring writers who were done with the early how-to guides. Folks who know ideas are easy but haven't yet figured out their particular toolkit. Each book would showcase the *craft* behind the story, rather than hiding behind the mythology of muses and inspiration and creative flow.

The Short Fiction Lab stories were my first attempt to deliver on this concept.

And, dear reader, I failed badly.

This flies against the narratives built up around creativity, muses, and genius, of course. Pick any narrative about an artist with an idea—whether fictional or journalistic—and it will conflate the combination of inspiration and burning passion with fantastic success. Thus, when we fail, it's tempting to lay blame at the feet of the muse. After all, if you brought the passion and failed, surely the source of that failure was a lack of innovation and genius in your inspiration?

More experienced writers acknowledge their process is rife with chances to screw up. Our passion comes up against the limitations around a project: the available time, our current skill set, our network, our resources, and the mental bandwidth we can devote to a particular concept while satisfying the myriad commitments we have outside of writing. The most unacknowledged factor contributing to literary success is often privilege—the ability to buy yourself the freedom to execute an idea (and to have the project fail without adverse effects on your life). Whether that privilege stems from wealth, gender, or some other issue, our circumstances always shape the projects we finish (or don't).

The first editions of the Short Fiction Lab series fell shy of my intentions, but they were the best iteration of the concept I could accomplish at the time.

I don't regret putting them out into the world—I'll happily write and fail if the alternative is letting an idea sit fallow—but the frisson that drove me to create the series fizzled out rather than reaching a satisfying endpoint. Much as I enjoyed producing stories, the accompanying author notes didn't resonate with the insights I hoped. Five releases in, I begrudgingly acknowledged I lacked the time and the toolkit to deliver at the level I dreamt of and set the series aside.

This, too, holds an important lesson: sometimes, a weak execution reveals flaws you can shore up in future iterations. In fact, I'd argue failure is integral to the process. Embrace your willingness to fail, because the ability to try, then regroup, *then* forge ahead to the next project is often far more essential to a writer's career than any muse-driven ideation.

This shouldn't be a source of frustration, but a cause for celebration: if success isn't depending on having a great idea, there's always something *you* can do in order to chase it down. Given the choice between ceding control to the muses or guiding my own destiny, I'll always take the latter.[9]

The frisson driving the Short Fiction Lab series is straightforward, but *gloriously* ambitious: write a series that changes the way we talk about creativity from the better. Shatter the primacy of the "great idea" and showcase the craft.

The first editions failed, but in that failure, I saw an iteration that brought me closer to my goals. Stories accompanied by essays, rather than author notes. An ongoing interrogation of my process, embracing success and defeat as I go along.

It's a big job, but I figure we can take it one story at a time, and my circumstances here in 2023 are very different to 2019.

Once again, it's time to re-light the fuse and hope for an earth-shattering kaboom.

Peter M. Ball
Brisbane, January, 2023

Thank you for reading *The Early Experiments*. I hope you loved these stories and the glimpse behind the scenes, and the Short Fiction Lab continues in *Winged, With Sharp Teeth*. Featuring a short story about winged crocodiles and young lovers, plus an essay on the permeable nature of success in writing.

Read Winged, With Sharp Teeth now

If you dig short stories, be sure to check out my ongoing magazine, Eclectic Projects, which features a blend of short fiction and non-fiction every month. It shares a very similar philosophy to the Short Fiction Lab books, growing out of my monthly Patreon where a community of readers and writers get new work and behind-the-scenes details.

Read Issue 1 of Eclectic Projects today

Want to be the first to know about upcoming releases? Just sign up for my newsletter and get the latest news, deals, and more. Sign up here: www.PeterMBall.com/newsletter

---

1. You can find me writing about it at http://www.petermball.com/some-ideas-about-ideas/
2. This exposure to models and systems is a huge part of the reason new writers are encouraged to read.
3. Merely the most recent example of an archetype established by Jessica Fletcher in *Murder, She Wrote*.
4. Equally, there's a legacy of authors positioned as aspiring authors whose inability to find success or publication has everything to do with their lack of originality and talent, positioning their failure as a by-product of their not-worthy-of-genius status.
5. I should note an author's goals and ambitions are shaped by a variety of intersectional issues and the current circumstances of their career.
6. In these instances, it's often useful to have a longer discussion about the way we position books and authors within our culture, and how those positions shift. Countless prolific authors of popular fiction, from Raymond Chandler to Stephen King to Nora Roberts, have found them repositioned as 'respectable' writers in the latter stages of their career. Last long enough and folk will write PhD dissertations about your work, if only because your early fans find new careers as literary tastemakers.
7. Frisson: a sudden feeling of excitement or fear that generates an aesthetic shiver or goosebumps, especially when anticipating something yet to happen. I can work with both fear or excitement as a starting point.

8. My father had been living with Parkinson's for over a decade, at the time, and was soon to be diagnosed with early stage dementia. Other friends were dealing with similar things.
9. Which is not to say that writers are in control of *everything* — networks and the market will influence success and failure as often as anything else — but in a publishing landscape in which so many things are outside our control, let's not give up any aspect of our career that we don't have too.

ABOUT THE AUTHOR

PETER M. BALL is an author, publisher, and RPG gamer whose love of speculative fiction emerged after exposure to *The Hobbit*, *Star Wars*, David Lynch's *Dune*, and far too many games of *Dungeons and Dragons* before the age of 7. He's spent the bulk of his life working as a creative writing tutor, with brief stints as a performance poet, gaming convention organiser, online content developer, non-profit arts manager, GenreCon convenor, and d20 RPG publisher.

He's the author of the Miriam Aster series and the Keith Murphy Urban Fantasy Thrillers, three short story collections, and more stories, articles, poems, and RPG material than he'd care to count.

He's the brain-in-charge at Brain Jar Press, an aspiring mad scientist running publishing experiments through Eclectic Projects, and resides in Brisbane, Australia, with his partner and a very affectionate cat.

Find Peter Online at PeterMBall.com *or reach out to Peter on your favourite Social Media platforms:*

- patreon.com/PeterMBall
- facebook.com/PeterMBall
- instagram.com/PeterMBall
- tiktok.com/@petermball
- goodreads.com/PeterMBall
- amazon.com/Peter-M-Ball/e/B00QRZF37C
- bookbub.com/authors/peter-m-ball

ALSO BY PETER M. BALL

SHORT STORY COLLECTIONS

The Birdcage Heart & Other Strange Tales

Not Quite The End Of the World Just Yet: Short Stories & Strange Futures

These Strange & Magic Things: Short Stories

KEITH MURPHY URBAN FANTASY THRILLERS

Exile

Frost

Crusade

Local Heroes

Gold Coast Ragnarok (Omnibus)

MIRIAM ASTER NOVELLAS

Horn

Bleed

ESSAY COLLECTIONS

You Don't Want To Be Published & Other Things Nobody Tells You When You First Start Writing

CHAPBOOKS

Deeper Cuts: Night, Morning, Story & Impact

Gold Coast, 2002: Poems

JOIN THE ECLECTIC PROJECTS PATREON

Original Fiction Every Week

Want to join a great community of readers who receive original fiction every week? Sign up for the Eclectic Projects pattern for as little as a buck a month, and you'll receive early access to stories, ebooks, and more.

What are you waiting for?

Join us at patreon.com/PeterMBall.

www.ingramcontent.com/pod-product-compliance
Lightning Source LLC
Chambersburg PA
CBHW020133130526
44590CB00040B/608